How to work successfully with colleagues

*A Short Survival guide to Getting Along
in any Workplaces*

Emma W. Rose

Books On demand

© 2019 by Emma W. Rose
Edition : Books on Demand, 12/14, Rond-Point des
Champs-Elysées, 75008 Paris (France)
Impression : Books on Demand GmbH, Norderstedt,
(Germany).
ISBN : 9782322133918
Legal deposit : february 2019

Probably more people than you realize spend the majority of their time working with others in an employment-related situation. And, unless they're lucky, these individuals don't get to pick who their co-workers are.

Unfortunately, not everyone knows how to get along with others. This can cause all kinds of difficult situations, making it almost impossible to get through the day.

Working well with others is crucial in any situation. However, it's even more important in a workplace environment. Why? It boils down to things like efficiency, productivity and employee morale... just to name a few.

The size of the company or business you work for really doesn't matter. The rules are basically the same if you work with one other person or 1,000. Each individual deserves the same level of consideration.

During your job search, have you ever noticed the phrase "must work well with others" in the job description or on the application? If so, there's a very good reason for this. Employers do not want to hire individuals who don't work well with others. It typically causes problems right from the beginning.

Defining Others

In this case, "others" can be defined as everyone you come into contact with while on the job. Obviously, the answer is going to be different for everyone. However, it can include the boss, your co-workers, the customers or clients you interact with, any vendors you utilize, the HR team, maintenance or cleaning staff... the list goes on.

One of the main reasons it's so important to treat everyone equally is that you never know what a person might be able to help you with or do for you in the future. Of course, that means never taking advantage of that particular person's assistance or eagerness to help, under any circumstances.

Are you familiar with the expression "it's not what you know, it's who you know?" Think of it like this. Someone you don't interact with on a daily basis, but still consider a friendly acquaintance, could share a tip with you regarding a friend who happens to be hiring for a position you'd love to have. Without that tip, you wouldn't be aware of the opportunity. This scenario happens much more than you probably think. Just another reason to be considerate to everyone.

Another possibility is making a friend you wouldn't otherwise have. Diversity in the workplace is more commonplace than ever before. This gives individuals a much better chance of becoming friends with someone who isn't part of their everyday life. It might be someone who works in a different department or the person who maintains the office grounds. When it comes to meeting, and making a new friend, the possibilities are almost endless.

Why It Can Be Challenging to Work with Others

There are several reasons why it can be challenging to work with others. Many people have a tendency to bring their egos to their job site. It could be that these individuals are really self-conscious and unsure of themselves underneath. So, they use a big ego as a cover-up.

Quite honestly, grandstanding at work backfires more often than not. It creates resentment and bad feelings very quickly. When an employee doesn't work well with others, for whatever reason, chances are high that that person will end up getting terminated.

If this unbecoming behavior continues, the same person risks getting terminated over and over again until he or she finally finds a job where getting along with people doesn't matter. It's a sad scenario when you think about it. Don't let it happen to you!

Another challenging part of working with others is making an effort to avoid competition. If a fellow employee isn't getting along with you, it may be because of the competitive aspects of your job description and the fact that they're trying to beat you at something.

Yes, it's true that a bit of friendly competition can entice workers into improving their performance. However, bringing someone else's work performance up in order to get to them isn't going to do anything other than hurt their feelings. This can lead to a decrease in your own performance and could even cause you to think about moving on and finding a job elsewhere.

The Importance of Respect

If everyone on the job isn't being treated with respect, it can be bad for business. If you don't feel like you're being treated with respect at work, it can be extremely difficult to do your best. The same is true of your co-workers. They may not be able to perform their duties efficiently if and when their confidence has been put into check by a disrespectful co-worker.

A mutual respect between workers also helps to foster an environment of co-operation between members of the team. If you respect the people you work with, it's much easier to work with them toward achieving a goal. If you don't have any respect for your co-workers or their abilities, why would you count on them to help you out?

The best way for a team of employees to build a bond of mutual respect is through training and exercises meant to help everyone to get to know co-workers and their skills. It can be as simple an activity as having each team member share their name and parts of their job they feel they're best at.

In an environment where disrespectful behavior is common, conflict is more likely to break out between you and your co-workers. But, it's important that you don't let disrespectful behavior get to you and cause you to act the same way.

A dispute at work has a negative impact on both morale and overall productivity. If you feel like a co-worker isn't treating you with respect, talk to them about their behavior in a calm, respectful manner. If they aren't willing to discuss it, take the issue to your boss or supervisor.

Essential Skills and Habits You Need to Work with Others

There are numerous essential skills and habits you need in order to work well with others. Developing the proper habits, early on, helps put you on track to things like higher pay and leadership opportunities. Since more and more companies are making the decision to hire within, these things are more important than ever before.

Many of these things will probably seem obvious to you. However, if they were obvious to everyone, they wouldn't need to be listed. Please note, this isn't a complete list of the skills and habits you need to succeed, but it definitely gives you a good place to start. As you can probably see, a lot of these suggestions don't take much more effort than remembering them. There's no reason to panic and think you have to change your entire way of life.

Although these things may seem insignificant when you look at them separately, failing to do several of them adds up to a bigger problem. It really can mean the difference between keeping a job or getting fired. This is especially true in today's economy. With so many people actively looking for employment, employers generally find it very easy to fill their open positions.

Take Responsibility

It's always important to take responsibility for things that you do, especially when something goes wrong. No one is perfect. All but a few unrealistic employers realize that. If you make a mistake and claim that it wasn't your fault, not only are you not telling the truth, you're also giving the impression that you weren't in control of the situation.

By taking responsibility, you'll probably notice two things. Firstly, your co-workers will likely be more willing to help you correct the problem and help you to succeed. Secondly, these same individuals will be more comfortable around you, knowing that you are honest and will never place the blame on someone else.

Keep an Open Mind

Even in situations where you know you are 100 percent correct, it's always advisable to keep an open mind. This is especially true when you happen to be in a managerial position. Why? If you're never open to new or alternate ideas, you may come across as someone who knows it all. When this happens, people typically get defensive very quickly and it's downhill from there.

It's much more productive to show a little bit of humility and concern about truly finding the right answer for every issue and situation. Because everyone has a different problem-solving process, teamwork really has the potential to resolve issues and come up with great ideas much faster.

Honor Your Commitments

Always try to allow enough time to complete projects in a timely manner, even when something unexpected comes up. It's much better to give yourself more time than necessary to finish whenever you're working on, rather than to underestimate the time needed to complete the assignment. This way, you don't have to worry about disappointing your employer or your colleagues.

Go the extra mile. Always follow up on things, whenever possible. This accomplishes two things. One, it strengthens workplace relationships. Two, it provides you with important feedback regarding your performance.

Practice Proper Hygiene

Regardless of whether you're working with the public or in a back office, practicing proper hygiene is essential when you work with others. No one wants to be around someone who smells bad or looks like they slept in their clothing. This doesn't mean you have to dress like the rich and famous. It simply means to shower daily and come to work looking and smelling presentable.

If you're on a tight budget, consider purchasing clothing at local thrift stores. You can pick up great deals on clothing that's perfectly suitable for work. These stores typically stock a wide variety of business attire at fantastic prices. You just have to be there at the right time, which is on the days that the store gets deliveries.

Turn Off Your Phone

Almost everyone has a cell phone these days. If you work in a large office, constant ringing can be a major distraction. Unless you need your phone for work purposes, turn it off or put it away. Quickly reading a text message when someone is speaking to you is extremely rude. It gives the impression that your phone is more important than your job. Make a habit of checking your messages or making quick calls during your breaks or lunch period.

Share Credit

When applicable, sharing credit with your co-workers is a sure sign that you work well with others. Not only will that person or individuals like you even more than they did before, you'll probably gain a higher level of respect as well.

On the other hand, if you don't share credit when credit is due, you'll gain a reputation as someone who is selfish and out to sabotage everyone else in attempt to get ahead. If you happen to get away with this without anyone complaining, don't waste your time celebrating. In reality, the truth usually prevails and you won't get ahead - you may just find yourself in the unemployment line instead.

Don't Interrupt

Have you ever been in the middle of a conversation, only to be constantly interrupted? It's annoying, isn't it? For that reason, never be "the interrupter." Even if you have a great idea that you can't wait to share, wait until it's your turn to talk. Take a deep breath and relax. You'll be sharing your news or idea before you know it.

Here's a little secret. There are individuals who aren't all that impressed when you talk, regardless of how fantastic your idea. These people would much rather talk about themselves. So, when you let them do the talking first, it's a good way to get them to love you. After that, they may be all the more receptive to what you say.

Smile

The act of smiling is often referred to as a person's most powerful gesture. Science can back up the fact that individuals who smile often are not only happier, they're more successful as well. Even better - smiling doesn't cost you a penny. It's free to smile and watch the world (or at least the people you work with) smile right back at you.

It's interesting to note that some training modules for phone-related customer service positions requires agents to keep a small mirror by their phone. This way, the agent can make sure they're smiling when they speak to the customer. Believe it or not, the person at the other end of the receiver can usually hear the smile in the agent's voice. It makes for a much more pleasant interaction between the two, and many times higher sales.

Utilize Resources

Working well with others, to the best of your ability, sometimes involves utilizing resources. Depending on where you work and your job description, many companies provide all kinds of options for you to take advantage of.

These resources can be things like seminars, training sessions, fitness programs, no-cost safety equipment, mental health and family counseling, and more. If you run across a good resource you think would benefit your workplace environment and your co-workers, don't hesitate to mention it to your manager or boss. Who knows? You might even get a small reward or bonus for taking the initiative to recommend something that might help your company succeed.

Don't Be a Noise Maker

In the event your employer allows you to listen to music or something similar, don't be a noisemaker. Wear headphones or keep the volume at a non-distracting level. Remember, not everyone will have the same taste in music as you do. If your co-workers don't enjoy what they hear, you'll probably make it more difficult for them to concentrate and get their job done properly. The time to make noise is after the workday is done, unless you're a rock musician or an auctioneer.

Respect Boundaries

Your job might require you to share a space with your co-workers, whether it's a cubicle, office, or vehicle. If you are near others while you work, make sure that you respect their boundaries and encourage them to respect yours in return.

Try not to have phone calls about non-work-related matters if your cubicle mate is quietly focused on a project. Also, try not to divulge too much about your personal life, because this may be too much information for some people. These boundaries will differ from person to person, so if you aren't sure if you behavior is going to annoy your co-worker, it may be best to ask first.

Learn to Let Go

Once you've had a dispute with a co-worker, it can be difficult to get your relationship with them back to a state where you can work together effectively. If the dispute has been resolved, the best thing that you can do is move on to focus on work. Of course, your co-worker will have to focus on letting go too.

If they still seem upset over the issue, see if they're willing to talk about it. If they tell you why they're still not satisfied after the dispute was settled, do what you can to make things right between the two of you. If problems persist between the two of you, it may be best to inform your boss or supervisor.

Benefits of Working Effectively with Others

Teamwork is a wonderful thing. It may take everyone a bit of time to "get into the groove." But, when that happens it's beneficial to everyone involved - not to mention a success for the company. Here are a few benefits of working together on the job. Yes, it can be done!

Fills Voids

Working together typically fills voids. Not everyone has the same skills or education.

Teamwork allows people to contribute their separate knowledge to a project or problem as a whole.

It also come in extremely handy when someone is sick. If no one jumps in to do that person's job, everything could come to a standstill until the employee feels well enough to return to work. Companies lose business when they are functioning at less than 100 percent.

Promotes Healthy Competition

There's absolutely nothing wrong with a little bit of healthy competition in the workplace. This often leads to increased productivity, which is always encouraged. It's also an excellent motivator. Many times, when co-workers see their peers doing an excellent job, they want to do all they can to match (or even outdo) the performance.

Fosters Conflict Resolution

No matter how well you and your teammates work together as a group, there's always the chance of conflicts popping up now and again. There's no set-in-stone guarantee to avoid them completely. This is partly due to the fact that employees come from different backgrounds and have different styles of doing things. It's what makes the world and the workplace environment so interesting.

When conflicts present themselves, your team is then forced to come up with a resolution that best fits the situation. This is a very good skill to have under your belt, especially for those interested in future promotion opportunities.

Inspires Risk-Taking

You may not think that risk-taking is something that should be attempted on the job. However, there is such a thing as "healthy" risk-taking. Think of it like this. If you were working on a project by yourself and that project somehow failed, you would be responsible for the failure in its entirety.

On the other hand, if you're working as a team, your co-workers not only share ideas - they also share in the success or failure of the end result. In essence, teamwork gives everyone in the group the freedom to safely think outside of the box and really brainstorm new possibilities.

Boosts Efficiency

The more effectively a team of employees work together, the more work they'll be able to get done. Of course, having more people means being able to put forth more effort. But, a large team may actually get in each other's way if they are not working together effectively. Even if you don't work directly with a team, communicating effectively with other members of your organization helps to get things done as quickly as possible.

Establishes Trust

Finishing a project with co-workers does a lot to build a relationship with them. Once they actually help you to get things done, you'll know that you'll be able to rely on them again in the future. This feeling of trust will give you a level of safety that will make it much easier to work and share ideas with your co-workers.

On the other hand, if members of the team don't trust each other, they can make decisions that aren't good for the business in the long run. They may feel that they're the only member of the team they can actually get the job done, and therefore try to do the whole thing themselves. This could lead to a serious drop in efficiency, and potentially even bigger problems if the added strain causes this employee to make a mistake.

Training New Employees

If you're the one in charge of training new employees at the workplace, you have a major impact on their impression of the organization as a whole. If your training is effective, and you're there to assist as they need it, they'll see the company as helpful and a good place to work. But, if you don't provide them with the help they need, they aren't likely to build a positive relationship with the company. Here are a few things to keep in mind while training a new employee.

Focus on Building Strengths

As you work with a new hire, be on the lookout for areas where they excel and encourage them to build on their expertise. Not only will this encourage them to do a good job now, it will also set them up to get a promotion for a job that suits their skill sets in the future. In addition, ask them if they have any other strengths that they feel could help them get the job done. They may be able to help out the company in ways that you hadn't thought of beforehand.

Find Resources Online

There are a number of different learning programs available on the internet that are well-suited to many different companies and organizations. These courses typically include written instructions and instructional videos, as well as interactive components such as quizzes, puzzles, or even games. With such a wide variety available, you're bound to find a course for every department in your organization. All it takes is a bit of research.

Ask for Help

If you're having a hard time training new employees, it may be time to call in some help. Professional workplace training companies are out there and can help to educate your staff on a great number of things.

Typically, these groups come right to your place of work to administer their training. However, the assistance provided can prove to be pretty costly. In order to keep training costs to a minimum, think of your current staff. If any of them are exceptionally talented in one of the areas your training covers, ask them if they would be willing to spend some time with your trainees. They may be able to provide insights that would not have occurred to you.

Encourage Learning

It's hard to teach someone who doesn't want to listen to what you have to say. And, if your new employees aren't enthused about their new job, it can be difficult to train them on doing things effectively.

It's important that you spark an interest in your trainee to learn about their job, rather than simply tell them what to do. Make sure that they know that there's nothing wrong with asking questions, even if it's less about their job and more about the company as a whole. The more motivated they are to learn, the more their performance will improve as time goes on.

Give Them Something to Accomplish

After you've instructed your new employee on how to do their job, give them something to do so you can see how much of their training they can remember. Make sure that you monitor them as they do this, but try not to interfere too much unless they need help. Not only does it give you a good idea of what they've learned, it will also help them figure out how to apply it to their new job and help them to feel a sense of accomplishment.

Keep Things Fun

One of the biggest things you can do to help build a relationship between your trainee and your organization is to keep the tone light and friendly. This doesn't mean that you should make your training any less effective, or not work as hard during the training period. Just make sure to smile and keep things positive while you're working with them. Not only will it make learning their new job more pleasant for them, socializing with them now could also lead to you making a new friend in the future.

Types of Conflict in the Workplace

Much like conflict in our personal lives, conflict in the workplace can be difficult to avoid. Disputes among co-workers are often resolved among the parties involved without a hitch. However, it can sometimes be necessary to contact your human resources department or upper management to solve the problem if the dispute cannot be settled.

Part of handling conflict effectively is knowing what type of workplace conflict you're dealing with when the problem arises.

Leadership

A change of leadership such as a new supervisor or managerial staff can cause great conflict among employees. A sudden change in leadership can take some time getting used to, and may be stressful for you and your fellow co-workers in the process.

Drastic changes to leadership on the job takes people out of their comfort zone as they try to adjust to new rules and techniques, all while maintaining their workload. While it may seem daunting at first, much of this conflict can be avoided by providing a clear summary of any changes being made to rules in the workplace.

Conflicts of Character

Personality conflicts are some of the most common issues among co-workers. It can be difficult to pick up on social cues you're not accustomed to, or understand mannerisms that differ from your own and the people you are regularly in contact with. It's best to try not to take things so personally to avoid unnecessary confrontation.

If you can't think of a reason why your colleague is acting negatively toward you, you may have picked up on something that wasn't there. It's very unlikely that your co-worker arbitrarily decided to be rude to you.

It's Easier to Change Yourself Than to Change Others

Typically, change for the better is not easy for anyone to attain. You can't just snap your fingers or wave a magic wand and expect said changes to occur overnight. But, think of how great it would be if it was actually possible to accomplish the task!

However, keep this in mind. While it is possible to change yourself (with some effort involved - sometimes more than you're willing to put into it), it's extremely difficult to change others. More to the point, when you take time to think about it, do you really have that right?

It's hard to change a situation when you don't have back history and all of the facts. The same thing is true with a person. Until you've actually walked in someone's shoes, you don't know why that person acts the way they do. You may have a general idea, but generalities just aren't enough.

Whether you're at work or in another location, when the mood strikes you to want to change someone, try this instead. Think about things YOU can do to improve upon the issue. Coming right out and telling someone that you think they need to change is a sure way to initiate bad feelings between the two of you. Honestly, how would you feel if the tables were turned and someone was telling you that you need to alter the way you do things?

A good example of this relates to time management. You notice one of your co-workers is finding it difficult to stay on schedule in regards to completing a project. Instead of going to your manager with a complaint, why not ask the boss if there's some way that you can help the individual stay on track? You might even learn something new in the process.

If someone wants to change and asks for your help, it's a completely different matter. Doing all you can to assist them will help to ensure the transformation they hope to achieve. Sometimes, all the individual needs is a push in the right direction. Look at it this way: they'd probably do the same for you.

When to Call In the Boss

Many interpersonal conflicts at work can be solved without getting management involved. Your co-workers are adults, and you should be able to work out a reasonable outcome to any dispute you may have. While it is a good idea to keep your boss informed on what's going on between you and your co-workers, going to them with every issue may lead your fellow employees to believe that you aren't willing to listen to their side of the story.

However, if neither of you want to budge on the issue, it may be a good idea to get a supervisor or HR representative to mediate the conflict for you. Set up a time when you can all meet to work out the issue. With a neutral party involved to hear both sides of the story, they may be more inclined to curb whatever behavior was causing a problem.

Jobs for Introverts

If you happen to be an introvert, you can still take advantage of the guidance provided in this report. You just won't have to rely on it as frequently. If you're the shy type, consider applying for the following type of jobs. If you don't find one right away, don't give up. They are out there.

Animal Care

If you love animals, think about getting a job working at a veterinarian's office, animal shelter or even a pet store. Although the pay is lower than many other employment opportunities, the majority of the time will be spent working with the animals themselves. Leave the interaction with humans to your extroverted co-workers.

Social Media Manager

At first, this may seem like a strange choice. Yes, the job requires interacting with people. But, since it's all done via the internet, you don't have to actually be face-to-face with the people who you're communicating with. With the ever-growing popularity of social platforms, there will likely always be a need for this "behind the scenes" managerial position.

Court Reporter

At the time of this writing, the Bureau of Labor Statistics indicates that the median income for a court reporter is just shy of $50,000 per year. Even though a court reporter is required to be in the courtroom, he or she has very little interaction with anyone. The only time speaking is required is when someone asks the individual to read back part of the court transcript.

Freelance Writer

Thanks to the popularity of the internet, freelance writing opportunities are seemingly everywhere. Better yet, you don't need a college degree to get started. If you can write in an interesting manner and have a basic grasp at grammar, clients are out there waiting for your assistance.

Typically, the only time you have to actually interact with someone is when you're discussing a potential job or have questions for a current client. Even then, just about everything can be done via email.

Translator

If you speak one or more foreign languages, why not put this knowledge to additional use? A translator's job is simply to convert written documents or audio recordings from one language to another. No additional involvement from co-workers required.

Other possible options, with limited human interaction, include the following:

- Truck driver or delivery person
- Security guard
- Bookkeeper
- Landscaper
- Janitor
- Lab technician or researcher
- Artist
- Graphic designer

For more ideas, take an hour or so to do an online search. You'll probably be surprised by the employment suggestions for people who prefer to limit interaction with co-workers.

This information is just a small sample of things you can do to help ensure that you always work well with others, regardless of your job description or company position. Obviously, the easier it is for you to interact with co-workers and customers, the higher the chances of getting a raise or promotion.

You may have to work on some of these things before they begin to feel like second nature. The good news is that if that's the case, it's totally ok. Don't beat yourself up about it. There is no such thing as a perfect employee, no matter how much education or experience in the field he or she happens to have.

In any job, two of the most important traits to possess are diligence and honesty. As long as you exhibit both of these qualities, there's a good chance you'll succeed and, better yet, feel good about doing so.

Just like there is no perfect employee, there is no perfect job or set of co-workers. There will probably be times you feel frustrated by both, which is perfectly natural. During those periods, do all you can to remain positive about the situation.

Being positive is a choice you make. It doesn't only hinge on the good things that happen to you. If you remain positive even when things aren't the best, your co-workers will be more likely to pick up on your attitude and try to match it.

Some people are more introverted and prefer to work alone. If you fall into this category, that's ok too. As long as you can find work you're happy doing, that's the most important thing. However, you may want to consider this. By practicing some of the suggestions in this report, you may slowly find yourself becoming a little more extroverted.

If and when that happens and you find yourself feeling more comfortable around people, it may be time to make an attempt to expand your employment horizons. This new feeling of confidence won't happen overnight. But, with practice in patience, you may eventually find yourself wanting to work with others. And, there's certainly nothing wrong with that.

In closing, keep the following motivational quotes in mind. Better yet, write each of them on a Post-it note and stick them around your workstation. Remember, motivation is contagious. Why not help to spread around and make your work environment a friendlier and more productive place. Your co-workers will undoubtedly thank you for it!

"Always do your best. Don't stop just because someone doesn't give you credit."
~ Mary Rosen

"Work joyfully and peacefully, knowing that right thoughts and right efforts will inevitably bring about right results."
~ James Allen

"The best way to appreciate your job is to imagine yourself without one."
~ Oscar Wilde